WEDDING MUSIC
I. ARIA

1st Violin
B-458

G.F. HANDEL

1st Violin

II. BRIDAL CHORUS

(from "Lohengrin")

R. WAGNER

Con moto moderato

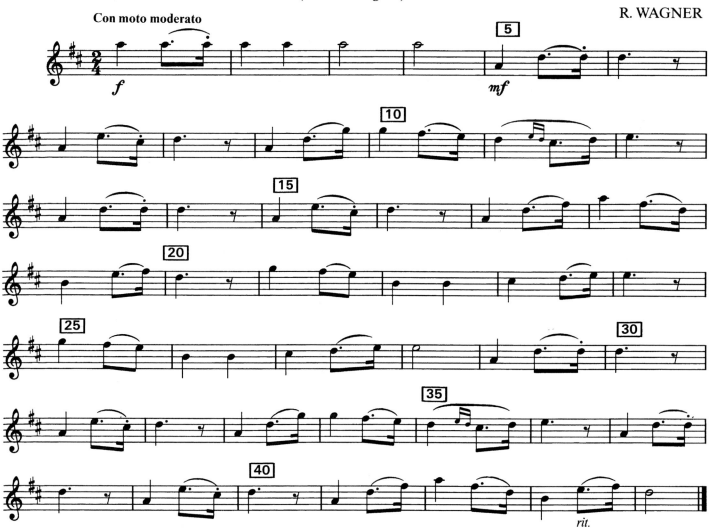

WEDDING MARCH

(from "A Midsummer Night's Dream")

F. MENDELSSOHN

Allegro vivace

IV. TRUMPET VOLUNTARY

J. CLARK

B-458

V. WINTER
(slow movement)

A. VIVALDI

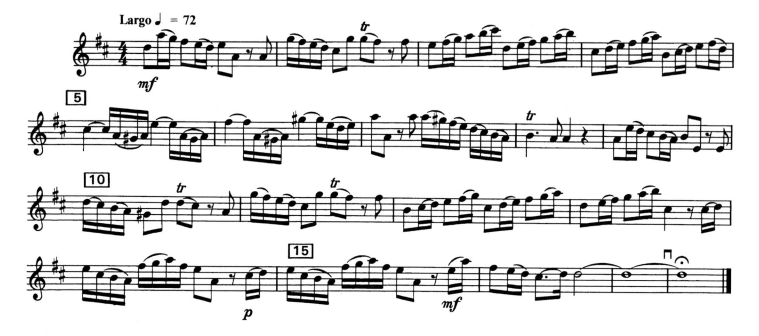

VI. RIGAUDON

A. CAMPRA

VII. THEME FROM 1ST SYMPHONY

J. BRAHMS

VIII. MARCH
(from "Marriage of Figaro")

W.A. MOZART

IX. TRUMPET TUNE

H. PURCELL

X. CANON

J. PACHELBEL

XI. JESU, JOY OF MAN'S DESIRING

J.S. BACH

B-458

XII. WINTER
(From 1st movement)

A. VIVALDI

Allegro non molto (♩ = 116)

B-458